A TABLE of GRACE

STORIES AND RECIPES
TO NOURISH THE HEART

ALDA ELLIS

HARVEST HOUSE PUBLISHERS
EUGENE, OREGON

A Table of Grace

Published by Harvest House Publishers

Eugene, Oregon 97402

Library of Congress Cataloging-in-Publication Data

Ellis, Alda, 1952-
   A table of grace / Alda Ellis.
      p. cm.
   ISBN 0-7369-0521-9
   1. Cookery, American. I. Title.

   TX715 .E4658 2001
   641.5973--dc21

                       00-059751

Artwork which appears in this book is from
the personal collection of Alda Ellis.

Design and Production by Left Coast Design, Portland, Oregon

Printed in China

01 02 03 04 05 06 07 08 09 10 / IM / 10 9 8 7 6 5 4 3 2 1

Dedication

To my sister, Cheryl Johnson,
for helping me uncover some of our mother's
well-kept secret recipes. Thank you for sharing
your warm thoughts and memorable moments
as you so gracefully carry on the traditions
of our family and help to make the
memories of tomorrow.

Contents

And where we love is home,
Home that our feet may leave,
But not our hearts.
The chain may lengthen,
But it never parts.

OLIVER WENDELL HOLMES

Come Gather 'Round Our Table

The beautiful, clear mountain lake just beyond our back door is a source of inspiration to my husband, Buddy. Late in the evening when all is quiet, he casts out his sweeping curve of fishing line time and time again, waiting for the tug on the other end of the line. Sometimes he patiently sits and watches the cork bob up and down as the sun fades behind the mountain cedars. When our son Samuel was little, he used to ask, "Daddy, why are you still fishing when you haven't caught any fish at all?"

In the long shadows of the evening, my husband answered, "It isn't the fish I enjoy; it's the fishing."

And so it is with me and the food on my table. The food may nourish my body, but it is the act of coming together and the warmth of the conversation that so nourishes my heart and soul.

Most days at four o'clock, I don't know "what's for dinner," but I do know that soon my husband, my two sons, my eighty-eight-year-old father, and I will be seated 'round our table to renew our bond of family. Sometimes our dinner table is outside on the patio. Most of the time it is in the kitchen beside a window that looks out on a hundred-year-old oak tree. Yet where our dinner is eaten isn't what matters. What matters is that we come together as a family at the end of the day. The television is off and the conversation is on. We may be having leftovers from the night before or grand holiday fare, but we can always count on the warmth of conversation and togetherness.

> It is the warmth of the conversation as well as the warmth of the food.
>
> ALDA

Nutrition is not just about feeding our bodies. It completes the circle of body and spirit. When I travel around the country, I become physically as well as mentally tired. Coming home from my trip to my kitchen table restores my spirit. My connection with my family is renewed as we enjoy simple, nourishing comfort foods.

My mother was the person in my life who set the example of coming together for meals at the end of the day. We sat down to so many meals of good, simple comfort food, and Mother always gave those meals a sense of style. The table was neatly set, with place mats, forks, spoons, knives, and napkins crisply folded on the diagonal. Actually, setting the table was my job—a chore I disliked at the time—but now I realize that Mother was giving me more than just a job to do. She was giving me a tradition of ritual. My other job was to get four shiny, polka-dot glasses down off the shelf, fill them with ice and tea, and place them next to the plates on the table. Now, in my own home, I take Mother's polka-dot glasses down off the shelf, fill them with ice and tea, and warmly recall my mother's cooking and my childhood meals.

My sister, Cheryl, and I each have our own favorite recipes that Mom made. We both loved her Springtime Salad, which was just mashed potatoes embellished with chopped green onions, a chopped, hard-boiled egg, and crumbled bacon. So easy, yet so pretty and oh-so-good. Cheryl adored Mother's Fried Chicken and Milk Gravy. My favorites were the Polka-Dot Cookies and Lemon Freeze that we ate for dessert. It is easy for both my sister and me to recall the delicious smells that wafted from the kitchen and the image of Mother cooking with her half-apron tied over her outfit. I just wish I'd told her more often how good her cooking was! I think of her as my own family now gathers 'round our table of grace.

SOUTHERN-FRIED CHICKEN Serves: 4

Our traditional Sunday dinner was usually Mother's fried chicken. Right after I was married I tried to impress my new husband with the same meal, but I had never ever fried a chicken before. I think he quickly figured that out, for as I—wearing my new pink Rubbermaid gloves—was rolling the chicken in flour, he was rolling with laughter. Twenty-five years later we are still married, and, with a little practice, I have learned the art of frying a chicken, Southern-style.

Cut up 1 large fryer. Sprinkle with salt and pepper. Marinate the pieces in sweet milk for at least one hour. (That's the secret!) Place 3 cups of flour in a brown paper bag. Drop the chicken pieces into the bag one at a time, shaking the bag vigorously to cover each piece in flour. Fry in hot shortening, always using an iron skillet.

SPRINGTIME MASHED POTATOES

Serves: 6

> 6 large red potatoes
> 2 cups boiling water
> 1/2 stick butter
> 1 cup milk
> 1 1/2 teaspoons salt
> dash black pepper
> 2 hard-boiled eggs, fincly chopped
> 4 green onions, chopped
> crumbled bacon

Wash the potatoes and peel them close to the skin. Slice into 3/4-inch thick pieces. Pour water into a heavy saucepan and bring to a boil. Add unsalted potatoes. Boil 20-30 minutes on medium heat until fork-tender. Drain the cooked potatoes and set the liquid aside. Mash potatoes with a potato masher. (I love to use my mother's red-handled one.) Add the cooking water back into the potatoes along with butter, part of the milk, salt, and pepper. Add the rest of the milk if needed. Fold in eggs and onions. Sprinkle crumbled bacon on top. Serve hot.

LEMON FREEZE

Serves: 8

Crust:

> 2 cups graham cracker crumbs
> 1/2 cup pecans, finely chopped
> 4 tablespoons sugar
> 8 tablespoons butter, melted

Mix dry ingredients, then slowly add melted butter, mixing well. Press into the bottom of a buttered 9" x 12" pan. Bake at 350 degrees for 10 minutes. Cool before filling.

Filling:

> 1 box lemon Jell-O
> 1 cup hot water
> 1 cup cold water
> 8 ounces cream cheese
> 1 cup sugar
> 1 14-ounce can sweetened condensed milk, chilled

Dissolve lemon Jell-O with hot water, then add cold water. Set aside. In a large mixing bowl, beat cream cheese with sugar. Fold in condensed milk and Jell-O mixture. Pour into crust and freeze approximately 6 hours before serving.

POLKA-DOT COOKIES *Makes: 18 cookies*

My sister went through hundreds of recipes Mother had clipped and saved in order to find her recipe for Polka-Dot Cookies. Some recipes were neatly written on index cards and listed the date and whom the recipe was from, while others were torn from the pages of magazines or hurriedly scribbled on envelope backs. This one was worth hunting for!

2 1/4 cups regular flour, sifted
3/4 teaspoon baking soda
1/2 teaspoon salt
1 cup (2 sticks) butter
1 cup dark brown sugar, firmly packed
1/2 cup granulated sugar
2 eggs
1 1/2 teaspoons vanilla
1 6-ounce package
    butterscotch pieces
1 cup tiny marshmallows

Measure flour, soda, and salt into sifter. In a large bowl, cream butter with sugar until fluffy. Beat in eggs and vanilla. Sift in flour mixture, 1/3 at a time, blending well. Stir in butterscotch pieces. Drop dough, approximately 1/4 cupful at a time, 6 inches apart on a large cookie sheet. Spread each drop into a 4-inch round. Bake at 375 degrees for 10 minutes. Place several marshmallows on top of each cookie. Bake 1-2 minutes longer or just until the marshmallows melt. Cool on a wire rack.

Note: Mother always made a double batch of these cookies, as they never seemed to last very long in our household! Sometimes I make them for my family and serve them with ice cream and fresh fruit. You can also put them in a pretty box and tie it with polka-dot ribbon for a most welcome gift.

O Lord, that lends me life, lend me a
heart replete with thankfulness.

SHAKESPEARE

On Saying Grace

Whether looking for a brand-new dish or trying to remember how to make an old favorite, it is evident that cooking and eating at home enriches our daily lives. It seems that every woman's magazine on the supermarket rack is loaded with recipes for how to cook this or that. I have even been known to take cookbooks to bed with me for my nightly reading!

Not only are the preparing, cooking, and eating of food important, but the act of coming together at mealtime helps families to strengthen their relationships and connections. The family dinner is indeed a legacy to be passed on from one generation to the next. I believe that it is more important for our children to know who the head of the family is than who the head of the country is. So many positive things begin while seated at the dinner table—respect, good communication skills, proper table manners, the humble thanking of God for our blessings.

Most nights, the meal on our family table is quite simple. Sometimes we have a friend or special guest eating with us, but most nights just our immediate family gathers together. "Our family" consists of three generations, for as of recently my daddy is always with us for our evening meal. When we are all seated 'round the table, a brief silence quiets the noisy chatter and a genuine gratitude of the heart can be felt when my father blesses our food with a prayer. Ever since we lost my mother two years ago, I think it has helped all of our hearts to heal as we bow our heads and acknowledge our abundance of blessings.

> *I value this delicious home feeling as one of the choicest gifts a parent can bestow.*
>
> WASHINGTON IRVING

It seems to me that laughter is also an important ingredient to have at the table, for it makes coming together at the end of the day an event to look forward to. We are always guaranteed a good laugh at our dinner table. Our oldest son, Mason, attends an all-boys high school. During our evening meal, we like to ask him to share a funny story of what happened at school that day, and most nights he is able to oblige us. We call Mason our dinner entertainment for, as you might imagine, the boys are always up to something! He keeps the laughter at our table flowing.

The dinner table is also a place for listening. When I

was little, Mother used to remind me that God gave us two ears and one mouth. Remembering her advice, I make an effort to listen to what is going on in the day-to-day lives of my sons. Our mornings are usually hectic, on-the-run times. The boys are in school most of the day and I am working, so our schedule leaves very little time for uninterrupted listening. Seizing those teachable moments, I must remember that it is not so important that we talk to each other, but that we also *listen* to each other.

Coming together at the end of the day with our family and sharing our blessings, concerns, and joys help to bind our family ties. And lessons acted upon are worth far more than words ever spoken.

The most valuable gift I can give my sons is that of a good example. Sometimes we take turns saying grace before a meal so that the boys will become comfortable doing so. As a mother, the things my boys are thankful for often amaze—and amuse—me. "Not getting my name on the board for talking" is sometimes Samuel's daily blessing. Mason's might be, "Thank You for the good grade on my algebra test."

I know that someday my father will not be seated at our table to say his few words of grace: "Bless this food...bless those our duty to pray for." Someday my husband will inherit this daily honor. In raising my two sons, it is my wish that they take with them the memory of these days and one day begin in their own homes a table of grace.

> *Be present at our table, Lord*
> *Be here and every where adored*
> *Thy people bless and*
> *grant that we*
> *May feast in fellowship*
> *with Thee.*
>
> A WESLEYAN GRACE

> *Here are fruits, flowers, leaves*
> *and branches...here is my heart....*
>
> VERLAINE

Gatherings

Sharing an evening with good food and good friends is very rewarding. Opening up our homes with warm hospitality, and a little— or a lot—of festive spirit is one of the keys to entertaining. I love the saying, "We make a living by what we get. We make a life by what we give." There's so much truth to that! The things that count most in life simply cannot be counted.

My friend Demi once surprised me on my birthday with a dinner party in her home. I have been to much fancier parties, but I have never attended one more memorable, for Demi possesses the secret to good entertaining. The fire was lit in the fireplace to ward off the cold October chill. The smell of her homemade marinara sauce greeted us at the door and a handful of fresh daisies were a feast for my eyes. Ten years later, I still remember the most wonderful, homemade Mississippi Mud Cake she served. Gathered around her oak table with a few other friends, she gave me the best-ever birthday present—the treat of a delicious meal and the joy of being surrounded by those I loved in the warmth and comfort of her home.

Living in the country with room to spare, we have large gatherings in our home fairly often, yet they are always quite comfortable for there is always an extra chair. I have learned to prepare dishes that can stretch. That way, if a few more guests than expected drop by, they will only add to the joy of the day.

> *I shall pass through this world but once. Any good, therefore, that I can do or any kindness that I can show to any human being; let me do it now. Let me not defer nor neglect it, for I shall not pass this way again.*
>
> GANDHI

This year, I planned and prepared our traditional Easter dinner like I always do. However, the day before the holiday arrived, it seemed as if all of our plans were falling through. Most of our extended family always gathered together on this day, but it seemed that one by one, something was happening to prevent each person from coming. However, I decided to prepare as if everyone were coming. Ham could be frozen if needed, baked beans could always be reheated, and a big batch of potato salad was easy to make—and to eat! In the back of my mind, I reasoned that leftovers would be wonderful, for it would be so nice to put together easy meals to begin the week.

To my glad surprise, when it came time for the Easter dinner, everyone who had been invited ended up being able to come—even the retired couple down the road whom my husband forgot to tell me he had invited! Thanks to my optimistic thinking, there was plenty of food for everyone that day.

> *Remember to show hospitality. There are some who, by doing so, have entertained angels without knowing it.*
>
> THE BOOK OF HEBREWS

Every Easter, we look forward to the traditional egg hunt on the lawn. After dinner we hide plastic Easter eggs filled with candy and coins for the little ones to find. Sometimes not all of the eggs are found until early in the summer when my husband mows the lawn. The lawnmower usually finds at least two colorful eggs!

Springtime has always been a time of celebration for our family with Easter dinner, graduation parties, Mother's Day luncheons, bridal parties, and garden parties. One of the sweetest garden parties I have ever been to was given by my friend JoAnn in celebration of her peonies in bloom. She invited my son Samuel and me along with other friends and neighbors to mingle through her flowering garden late in the day. Before we left for the party, Samuel asked me, "Mama, what do you do at a garden party?" Because Samuel has always had a garden of his very own and has enjoyed showing me how the plants in it changed on a daily basis, I knew he would understand how JoAnn wanted to share her own garden's glory with us.

We admired JoAnn's flower gardens in her well-manicured yard and delighted in the table laden with food. As the evening sun began to pull the shadows long, JoAnn lit the candles for the evening. At that wonderful party, I was able to renew old friendships, make new acquaintances, enjoy the company of my son, and feast on the sight of beautiful flowers and the taste of delicious food. JoAnn had given us more than a party—she'd given us the lasting gift of hospitality.

> *The heart is happiest when it beats for others.*
> AUTHOR UNKNOWN

True hospitality comes from the heart as we open the doors of our homes and set our tables to create a warm and welcoming spot for family and friends. Even the most appropriate of etiquette may fall short if the hostess fails to bestow the gift of hospitality upon her guests. It is a gift of time in the midst of our busy schedules that simply says, "Welcome into our day; welcome into our home."

With simple menus and recipes, you can enjoy the company of friends and family and develop your own sense of entertaining style with the utmost of confidence. Add a dash of enthusiasm, and you've created a most memorable time for all!

Entertaining may sound difficult, but it is actually quite easy. It simply boils down to making your guests feel special, comfortable, and welcome as they gather 'round your table of grace.

*Forget yourself for others,
and others will not
forget you.*

AUTHOR UNKNOWN

SENSE AND SENSIBILITY

When entertaining, I always keep a checklist in the back of my mind for making all of the senses feel welcome.

THE SENSE OF TASTE

It's a good rule of thumb to offer something to eat and something to drink appropriate for the season. When it is cool outside, offer a warm drink. When it is hot outside, a cool glass of refreshment is fitting. The food you serve need not be elaborate fare, for sometimes simplest is best—fresh fruit, a wedge of sharp cheddar cheese, shortbread cookies, and tea or coffee to drink. Figs are a favorite of mine when they are in season. A few figs displayed on an ironstone platter look quite elegant. Ice water is lovely with a slice of lemon. Or try serving ginger ale with a strawberry perched on the rim of the glass. When it is cold outside, it's hard to top a mug of hot chocolate with marshmallows floating on top.

THE SENSE OF SMELL

Smell is perhaps the strongest of our senses. Imagine an aromatic meal cooking on the stove, warm apple cider, and scented candles. And you can be creative when it comes to scents. When frost is on the pumpkin, potpourri, pomanders, and room sprays can make your home smell as beautiful as it looks. Scents surround us all throughout the day, and a heightened aroma of certain fragrances can create an atmosphere, set a mood, or simply enhance our well-being.

THE SENSE OF HEARING

I always have classical music playing in the background of my home. Even if I am the only one in the house, it is still so serene and calming. You can choose other styles of music to match the event. I particularly like instrumental music, for it seems to quell any uncomfortable quiet and puts everyone at ease. When music plays, conversation flows. Try light jazz for an evening of seafood, Frank Sinatra for a Manhattan-style buffet, or country-western for a barbecue.

On the Fourth of July, my family and I always attend a gala affair. A most gracious man, George Fisher, hosts it. The food is always delicious, but the highlight of the evening is the music. When the musicians congregate on the porch, we all gather 'round. Sometimes George himself, with guitar in hand, joins in the bluegrass band with a funny song. The music is most memorable from one year to the next.

If I am not sure just what to play at one of our gatherings, I usually put on Handel's *Water Music*, a Strauss waltz, or Pachelbel's *Canon in D*, for these pieces always seem appropriate. Keep the music on the CD or tape player fairly low so that lively conversation is at ease.

If you have a piano, invite someone to play it at your party, especially as guests arrive. It gives the party an instant warm and festive atmosphere and serves as an icebreaker for guests as they arrive.

THE SENSE OF SIGHT

Well-thought-out lighting is most important for any planned party or even for an impromptu visit from a friend. Conversation is cozier with lights turned lower, for overhead lighting is usually quite harsh. We have had dimmer switches installed in our home. This is especially wonderful in the dining room, when candlelight is sometimes not quite enough to dine by. Little table lamps or lamps on the bookshelf, elongated picture lights over a framed piece of art, and of course candlelight can give any room a soft, warm ambience.

An attractively set table is a feast for the eyes as well as a perfect way to set the mood. Keeping this in mind, I remember to garnish the meals I serve. Recently I watched an author promote her new cookbook on a television cooking show. The pie she baked sounded good as she read off the list of ingredients and began to prepare it. But when she offered the pie as a finished product, it looked very drab and uninteresting, as it had not been garnished in any way. A sprig of mint, a fresh pansy, a twisted slice of orange, a sliced strawberry, or an edible orange nasturtium—these are those touches of detail that say to your guest, "You are special." A small detail can add so much!

THE SENSE OF TOUCH

It seems to me that any gathering becomes a more lasting and memorable event if I send my guests home with a special treat. I always like for my guests to leave with something in their hand. It does not have to be a wrapped present, and a guest need never feel obligated to return the favor. Instead, it is a gift of thoughtfulness, such as a bottle of herbed vinegar, a homemade candle, a cutting from my flower garden, or a couple of fresh-baked cookies wrapped in cellophane and tied with curled ribbon. I recently enjoyed using a bottle of barbecue sauce that a friend had given me as a party favor. It brought to mind all over again her most wonderful Atlanta dinner party.

EDIBLE FLOWER GARNISHES

Some of these flowers look quite pretty simply as they are, while crystallizing may embellish others. To crystallize, brush the petals lightly with egg white, then sprinkle with sugar over wax paper. Let air dry and store in an airtight container until ready to use. Imagine frosted pink rose petals and frosted purple grapes...so pretty together!

> Calendula
> Dandelion
> Lavender
> Marigold
> Nasturtium
> Pansy
> Rose
> Violet

MISSISSIPPI MUD CAKE *Serves: 12*

1 cup melted butter
2 cups sugar
4 eggs, beaten
1 1/2 cups flour
1/3 cup cocoa
1 cup broken pecan pieces
1 cup coconut
1 7-ounce jar marshmallow cream

Mix butter, sugar, and eggs together. Add flour and cocoa, mixing well. Fold in pecan pieces and coconut. Bake at 350 degrees for 40 minutes in a well-greased 11" x 17" pan. Remove from oven and spread top with marshmallow cream. Let cool, then ice.

Icing:

1/3 cup cocoa
1/2 cup butter
1 box powdered sugar
1/2 cup milk
1 teaspoon vanilla
1 tablespoon flour

VEGETABLE GARNISHES

CARROT CURLS

With a vegetable peeler, slice the carrot lengthwise into long strips. Secure with a toothpick and place in ice water to crisp for several hours. Remove toothpick before serving.

RADISH ROSES

Make a thin slice through the top and bottom of the radish and discard the end pieces. From the top only, make four slices deep into the radish but not all the way through. Crosscut the radish with three additional cuts. Place the radishes in ice water for two hours or longer, and radish roses will bloom.

SCALLION TASSELS

Trim the very tip of the white root end of the scallion so that the layers are no longer held together. Leave the scallion greens about three inches long. With scissors, cut the greens into several long, slender strips, still held together. Drop the onion into a bowl of ice water for two hours and the tassel will form as the blades spread out.

TOMATO ROSES

Use a very sharp paring knife to make long, thin strips of tomato peel. Start wrapping the peel around itself. (It gets larger as it winds.) Place on a damp paper towel, then gently lay another damp paper towel over the tomato roses. Store them in the refrigerator until you are ready to use them.

NOT ON THE GUEST LIST

We entertain out-of-doors, especially in the spring and summer, and we always seem to attract flying, biting, stinging, uninvited guests! Through the years, I have invested in quite a few glass hurricane lamps and railroad reproduction lanterns to go along with some I have bought at tag sales and antique fairs. I fill them with citronella oil and place them around the pool, patio, and gardens. They provide a romantic glow in the evenings and they also keep away those pesky bugs so that we can enjoy our festive evenings all the more!

> *Strength of character may be acquired at work,*
> *but beauty of character is learned at home.*
> *There the affections are trained. There the*
> *gentle life reaches us, the true heaven live.*

HENRY DRUMMOND

My Grandmother's Table

When we were growing up, my sister and I would go with our parents on a two-hour car trip to my grandmother's house once a month. My grandmother's neighborhood—the neighborhood my mother grew up in—is only about four blocks square. Time has passed by this sleepy little town, for only a gas station and a post office are left from the turn-of-the-century building boom. The old general store, a bank, and a theater all line Front Street, but they now stand empty.

The house my mother was born in, where my grandmother lived, was next door to the little Methodist church. Grandmother's was a large white house on a tree-shaded lot where silver leaf maples lined the driveway and cascading thrift overflowed the flowerbed that lined the walk. Anyone passing by might not look twice, but I always looked up into the arms of the big maple that once held a rope and burlap bag swing. A flash of memory recalled the time my cousin let go of the rope and fell flat on her back. She was all right—it just scared the rest of us to death!

Walking up the steps to my grandmother's house, I noted the two candy-apple red motel chairs that waited patiently for a taker. I spent hours playing with paper dolls on the front porch and ate grape popsicles in the front porch swing. The huge glass-paned front door opened into a foyer looking onto the living room, where my grandfather's big overstuffed chair sat next to his smoking stand. A sofa covered in red and pink cabbage roses sank deep to its knees. In the center of the house was the dining room, and in the middle of the dining room stood the biggest, grandest table I had ever seen.

When we came to visit, my grandmother would have already set the table in anticipation of our arrival. A welcoming place for all, the ball-and-clawfoot table seated ten comfortably without any of the table leaves in. It was so much bigger than our table at home, which seated just four. I used to tell my grandmother how much I loved her table. The china and silverware atop crisply-ironed table linens seemed special too. Looking back, I don't think it was the actual *table* that I loved, but instead the gathering of aunts and uncles and cousins who lived nearby and who always came for dinner when we did. The memories of grown-ups lingering around the table long after the food was gone and of the laughter and concerns of a family together were

what I loved most. After the table was cleared, my aunt and I
would cut and sew doll clothes from Grandmother's fabric scraps,
or sometimes we'd play a card game where she always let me win.
That ever-so-grand table was to me a precious symbol of our
times together.

My grandmother and mother are both gone, and that table is
now the center of my own home. I love to have aunts, uncles, and
cousins gather 'round amid the fruit salads, cakes, and casseroles,
just as my grandmother did. I enjoy setting the places with my
wedding china and Grandmother's Depression glasses. The table
has hosted many wedding showers, baby showers, and holiday and
birthday celebrations. Many math papers have been pondered over
from our sons' favorite homework spot. The handing down of this
table was more than just a handing down of a piece of furniture.
It was a handing down of a family tradition of togetherness. And
I think that my grandmother
would be pleased if she
could see her table
today.

SWEET POTATO PIE *Serves: 8*

Certain recipes make you think of someone special. My grandmother was known for her sweet potato pie. Whenever we had dinner with her, we could always count on her sweet potato pie at the table! After traveling in the car, we sat down at her chrome and red Formica kitchen table and were immediately handed a slice of this delicious treat.

2 cups sweet potatoes,
  cooked and mashed
1/2 cup butter, softened
2 eggs, separated
1 cup brown sugar,
  firmly packed
1/4 teaspoon salt
1/2 teaspoon ground
  cinnamon
1/2 teaspoon nutmeg
1/4 teaspoon allspice
1/2 teaspoon ginger
1/2 cup milk
1/2 cup granulated sugar
1 unbaked 9-inch piecrust

Mix together sweet potatoes, butter, egg yolks, brown sugar, salt, and spices. Stir in milk and mix well. Beat the egg whites at room temperature with an electric mixer (at high speed, for about a minute) until stiff peaks form. Slowly add the granulated sugar, just a bit at a time. Continue beating to allow the stiff peaks to form. Fold the egg white mixture into the sweet potato mixture. Pour into unbaked piecrust. Bake at 400 degrees for 10 minutes, then reduce the heat to 350 degrees and bake for an additional 45 minutes.

LEMON MERINGUE PIE   *Serves: 8*

I asked my friend Debra what food made her think of home. She said it would always be Lemon Meringue Pie, for it was her father's favorite, and she lost her father several years ago. Now, when Debra's mother knows Debra is coming for a visit, she always makes Lemon Meringue Pie and they share their warm memories of a very special husband and father.

3 tablespoons cornstarch	3 large eggs, separated
1 1/4 cups sugar	1 1/2 cups boiling water
1/4 cup lemon juice	1 9-inch pie shell, prebaked
1 tablespoon grated lemon rind	6 tablespoons sugar

Combine cornstarch, 1 1/4 cups sugar, lemon juice, and lemon rind. Beat egg yolks and add to cornstarch mixture. Gradually add boiling water. Heat to boiling over direct heat, stirring constantly. Pour into pie shell after boiling gently for 4 minutes while stirring constantly. To make meringue, beat egg whites until stiff peaks form. Gradually beat in 6 tablespoons sugar. Spread meringue on top of pie. Bake in hot oven at 425 degrees for 4-5 minutes to brown meringue. Cool and refrigerate. Serve cold.

WILTED LETTUCE SALAD   *Serves: 4*

This recipe makes me think of home, for my mother would fix this salad in the summertime when it was just too hot to cook. The black metal oscillating fan sat on the kitchen stool as she worked nearby. The lettuce, green onions, and tomatoes were all from her summer garden, so it was quick to prepare. I like to make it when I'm in a hurry.

9 cups torn leaf lettuce
6 green onions, finely chopped
8 slices bacon
1/2 cup cider vinegar
3 tablespoons brown sugar
12 cherry tomatoes, cut in half
1 small can sliced black olives

In a large salad bowl, combine lettuce and onions. Microwave bacon until quite crisp. Pour bacon drippings into a 2-cup measuring cup. Add vinegar and brown sugar to bacon drippings. Bring to a boil in the microwave and stir after one minute. Drizzle over torn lettuce and onions. Add black olives and cherry tomatoes. Serve immediately.

MOM'S FOOLPROOF MERINGUE

1 tablespoon cornstarch
8 tablespoons sugar
1/3 cup water
dash of salt
3 large egg whites

In a small, heavy saucepan, stir together cornstarch, 2 tablespoons sugar, and water. Cook over medium heat for 2-3 minutes, stirring occasionally until the mixture comes to a simmer and thickens. Remove saucepan from heat. Using a large bowl, add the salt to the egg whites. With an electric mixer, beat at medium speed until soft peaks form. Add the cornstarch mixture and beat until creamy. Gradually beat in the remaining sugar and continue to beat for 6-8 minutes or until nice, soft peaks begin to form.

RAISIN PIE   *Serves: 8*

It just would not be Christmas without my husband's mother bringing us her gift of Raisin Pie. Mom is a wonderful cook and a wonderful mother-in-law. Her gift is also a gift of time and tradition, as she knows her son would be sorely disappointed without it! Taken straight from Mom's recipe, I share with you her legendary, made-from-scratch favorite pie.

- 3/4 cup sugar
- 1 teaspoon cinnamon
- 1/2 teaspoon ground cloves
- 1/2 teaspoon nutmeg
- 1/2 teaspoon salt
- 1/3 cup cornstarch
- 1 cup water
- 2 tablespoons vinegar
- 3 large egg yolks (save the whites for the meringue)
- 1 cup raisins
- 1 teaspoon pure vanilla extract
- 1 2/3 cups evaporated milk (large can)
- 1 9-inch pie shell, prebaked

Combine sugar, spices, salt, cornstarch, water, and vinegar. Cook over low heat until mixture thickens slightly. Stir constantly so it doesn't stick to pan. Mix raisins, egg yolk, and milk together. Stir a small amount of raisin mix into the cornstarch mix, stirring constantly. Add the remaining raisin mix and stir over low heat for several minutes, whisking until it thickens. Add vanilla. Stir over low heat 2-3 minutes longer, until mixture thickens again. Pour into cooled pie shell and top with meringue. Spread the meringue mixture over the raisin cream filling, making sure the meringue touches the edges of the crust all the way around. This will keep it from shrinking and leaving a gap as it browns. Bake 25-30 minutes in a preheated, 350 degree oven until the meringue is golden brown.

STAINED-GLASS WINDOW COOKIES · *Makes: 24*

Our turn-of-the-century home has a large dining room with the original mural intact. The mural is the focal point in the dining room, and it is appropriately called "Going Home." We have even kept the original color of paint for the walls and trim in this room. I wanted to show the grand old moldings around the dining room windows, which would be hidden with draperies. The year we moved in, I made intricate stained glass windows to let the light through without hiding any of the woodwork. It was a labor of love, and I just adore the way the light filters in through the colored glass. The year my father-in-law retired from his job, my husband and I hosted a party in our home for his friends and well-wishers. I made these cookies and served them on a large silver tray at the reception. (The cookies were so much easier to make than the windows!) They were all a success, for the windows, the cookies, and my sweet father-in-law were all pictured in the Sunday paper!

1 12-ounce package
  semi-sweet chocolate
  morsels
1/2 cup butter
1 6-ounce package miniature
  pastel-colored
  marshmallows
1/2 cup pecans, finely
  chopped
1 package shredded flake
  coconut

Melt chocolate and butter in top of a double boiler. Let cool. Fold in marshmallows and nuts. Form into logs and roll in coconut. Refrigerate. When ready to serve, cut into 1/4-inch slices and arrange on a serving tray.

RECEPTION CHEESE CRISPS

Makes: 24 wafers

>   1/2 cup butter
>   1 cup sharp cheddar cheese, finely grated
>   1 cup all-purpose flour
>   1 cup Rice Krispies cereal
>   6 shakes Tabasco sauce

Mix all ingredients together and form mixture into 1-inch balls. Mash with the tines of a fork. Imprint with the fork in the opposite direction to form a crisscross pattern. Bake at 400 degrees for 10 minutes. Cool on a wire rack.

Note: These taste best when served fresh, but they may also be placed in an air-tight container and frozen for later use.

SPINACH DIP

Of all her recipes, my sister is probably best known for her spinach dip. Christmas, birthdays, receptions, any potluck—she always makes this recipe. It is so good, and it's appropriate for all sorts of occasions. I always keep the ingredients stocked in my pantry in case my sister is not coming to a gathering and I need to make some quick dip!

>   1 10 ounce package frozen, chopped spinach
>   1 can sliced water chestnuts
>   2 cups sour cream (lowfat is fine)
>   3 tablespoons mayonnaise
>   1 package dry vegetable soup mix
>   4 green onions, finely chopped

Thaw and drain spinach. Drain water off water chestnuts and chop coarsely. Mix all ingredients together and chill. This is best if made the day before you plan to serve it, as the flavors will have sufficient time to blend. Serve with a heavy cracker, such as Triscuits.

DORA JO'S CREAM CHEESE CORN *Serves: 6*

I keep this recipe handy in my cookbook stand, for the memory of my longtime friend Dora Jo bringing this to me when I was just home from the hospital still warms my heart. She is a very fine cook, always entertaining and bringing something special with her to work for everyone to share.

    2 cans whole kernel corn, drained
    8 ounces cream cheese
    1/4 cup butter
    dash of Tabasco sauce

Soften cream cheese and butter. Add to corn and a dash of Tabasco sauce. Heat to cook through or heat in microwave. Salt and pepper to taste.

Note: For a party, Dora Jo likes to sauté green bell peppers in butter and add them to the recipe along with chopped pimento for festive color.

MASON'S SPINACH BALLS   *Makes: 70 balls*

Mason, my oldest son, has always loved to cook. Ever since he was big enough to stand up in a chair at the kitchen counter, he would help me make these spinach balls for our Christmas holidays. They can be made ahead of time and frozen and are especially nice to have on hand during the holidays when unexpected guests might arrive. Just thaw, microwave to warm, and serve.

1 10-ounce package frozen
    chopped spinach, thawed
    and cooked
1 large white onion,
    finely chopped
1 small package herb-seasoned
    stuffing mix

5 eggs
3/4 cup butter, melted
1/2 cup Parmesan cheese
1 tablespoon garlic salt
1/2 teaspoon pepper
1/4 cup imitation bacon bits

Drain spinach. Cook onion in a little extra butter until clear. In a large mixing bowl, mix all ingredients until evenly combined. Roll mixture into 1-inch balls in the palm of your hand. Place balls close to each other on a large cookie sheet. Bake at 350 degrees for 10 minutes.

FESTIVE FIGS

Fresh figs are obtainable in the summer months, usually, from the Farmer's Market and at grocery stores with wonderful produce sections. Of course, they are also available dried in sealed packages, but they do not taste anything like the fresh ones. I just love to shop at my Farmer's Market, for I enjoy seeing the hands that have planted and harvested what I am buying. Select firm, ripe figs that are free from bruises, blemishes, or mold. Purchase them in small quantities, buying only what you think you will use, for they are very perishable. Store them in the refrigerator. When you are ready to eat your figs, wash and drain them, then remove the stems. Serve figs whole or cut in half and serve with a little sugar on a dessert plate. Delicious!

For flowers that bloom about our feet;
For tender grass so fresh and sweet;
For song of bird and hum of bee;
For all things fair we hear and see,
Father in Heaven, we thank Thee!

RALPH WALDO EMERSON

———◦◉◦———

Come Gather at My Table in the Spring

rom the time I was a child, the ritual of teatime has been a source of pleasure and fascination for me. In the spring, especially, there are so many occasions that call for a tea party. Taking a moment from the cares of the day and enjoying porcelain country rose teacups, dainty little sandwiches, and genteel conversation—a tea party transports us almost instantly into a world where grace and politeness are still important.

It was a cold, wet spring when I was in London. Three friends and I were staying at a most charming hotel in the very heart of the city. A special treat for us was an invitation to the hotel's traditional four o'clock tea. There my friends and I were ushered into a charming drawing room that boasted a merry, crackling fire in the fireplace. The sofa was covered in soft green velvet, and we sunk down in comfy side chairs dressed in gathered tulle. The walls were awash in candlelight as the flames from the fire danced for us. Underneath vintage portraits, a table of abundance beckoned us to taste all sorts of teatime fare. Dainty porcelain plates spilled pecan scones, home-made orange preserves, dabs of Devonshire cream, and burnt sugar for our hot tea. This was the first time I had ever tasted burnt sugar. I couldn't believe how something so simple could taste so wonderful. I wanted to leave London with more than a pleasant time—I wanted to leave with the recipe for burnt sugar!

Offer a cup of kindness with a spring tea.

ALDA

One of the attendants, who called herself the "Queen of Tea," chatted with us. She was very knowledgeable about the different flavors of tea and even about the history of taking tea. Charming us with her English accent, she shared with us the secret to making burnt sugar. I scribbled it down on the back of a taxi receipt. It is so easy, yet it can make teatime so special, for it is simply delicious in a cup of hot tea. I even learned that I can make it ahead of time to keep on hand for when a special occasion arises.

So many people in our lives are special to us. One way to let them know how we feel is by hosting a Cup of Kindness spring tea. A spring tea is a nice way to return a favor, renew a friendship, offer a thank-you, or just let a friend know how much you appreciate her. As the school year winds down, this is a heartwarming way to let your child's teacher know how much you appreciate her hard work. It is an especially memorable event if offered for no particular reason at all—not for an anniversary, not for a birthday, but just to offer a cup of kindness!

A CUP OF KINDNESS TEA

MENU

ORANGE SPICE TEA WITH TEATIME BURNT SUGAR
GARDEN FRESH CUCUMBER SANDWICHES
SPRING ASPARAGUS ROLL-UPS
PECAN SCONES WITH DEVONSHIRE CREAM
LEMON BARS
CANDY STRAWBERRIES
TEA PARTY BUTTER COOKIES

Remember to consider memorable ways for serving the food. Three-tiered silver servers might not be in everyone's china closet, but stacking pedestal cake plates offer the same towering effect. Trays can be decorated with starched Battenburg lace napkins and fresh flowers. The sound of silver, the tinkling of crystal, and the ring of china cups add to the atmosphere of the party.

Party decorations in general can be quite easy, for all you really need is a centerpiece of fresh flowers. It doesn't necessarily have to be a professional florist arrangement, for it is fun to make your own. Sometimes I use whatever is in bloom in my cutting garden—sprigs of rosemary, lavender, and basil tucked into the greenery give an added touch of fragrance. For a smaller, more intimate tea, pedestal wine goblets filled with water and a single floating blossom are small enough to fit on a serving tray. Blooms such as camellias, pansies, and orchids are ideal for floating because of their short stems. Spotlighting an individual blossom in water adds drama to the table, for the water acts as a lens to magnify the flower. A pure white camellia floating in a crystal goblet looks so elegant upon a silver tray.

TEATIME BURNT SUGAR

1 cup sugar
softened butter

Line a large cookie sheet with heavy-duty foil. Spread the sugar evenly onto the baking sheet, leaving a 2-inch open border around the edges. With the softened butter, generously cover the border. Place the pan under the broiler and broil the sugar until it melts. Be careful not to let it burn. When the sugar turns a deep caramel color, remove the pan from the oven. Let it cool and break the sugar into several pieces. Place it in a Ziploc-type bag and pound it with a rolling pin to granulate the sugar again. Store in an airtight bag or container, for moisture will make it sticky. I like to serve Teatime Burnt Sugar in an antique sugar bowl with a pretty sugar spoon.

GARDEN FRESH CUCUMBER SANDWICHES

Makes: 48

1 teaspoon fresh dill, chopped
8 ounces cream cheese
1 large cucumber, grated
1 loaf white bread, thinly sliced
1 small onion, grated
1 cup mayonnaise

Spread each slice of bread with a thin coating of mayonnaise. Mix the cream cheese, dill, cucumber, onion, and mayonnaise, then spread onto bread to make sandwiches. Trim the crusts and cut each sandwich diagonally twice to form four small triangles.

SPRING ASPARAGUS ROLL-UPS

1 loaf sandwich bread, thinly sliced
2 cans whole asparagus stems (or fresh asparagus, if available)
2 green onions, finely chopped
1/2 cup butter, softened
Parmesan cheese
paprika

Steam asparagus, if you are using fresh, about 3-4 minutes over boiling water until tender. Drain asparagus and pat dry. Trim crusts off bread and spread with softened butter. Sprinkle with green onions on top of the butter. Place one spear of asparagus on each slice of bread and roll up. Place on a large cookie sheet and spread a little butter on top of each sandwich. Sprinkle with Parmesan cheese and paprika. Bake at 350 degrees for 15 minutes or until lightly toasted.

LEMON BARS   Makes: 35

2 sticks butter, softened
2 cups all-purpose flour
1 cup powdered sugar
4 large eggs
2 cups granulated sugar
6 tablespoons lemon juice
1 tablespoon flour
1/2 teaspoon baking powder

To make crust, mix butter, flour, and powdered sugar and press into a 10" x 14" cake pan. Bake at 325 degrees for 15 minutes. To make filling, slightly beat eggs in a large mixing bowl and add sugar, lemon juice, flour, and baking powder. Mix well and pour on top of crust. Bake at 325 degrees for 40-50 minutes. Remove from oven and sprinkle with additional powdered sugar. Cool and cut into 2-inch squares.

Note: If you lay a paper doily on the lemon bars before you sprinkle the sugar, you will have a pretty design when you lift the doily.

PECAN SCONES

Makes: 16

2 cups all-purpose flour
1/4 cup granulated sugar
1 tablespoon baking powder
1 teaspoon salt
3 tablespoons butter
3 tablespoons cream cheese
2/3 cup milk
1 large egg
1/2 cup pecans, chopped
extra milk to brush on top
extra sugar to sprinkle on top

Lightly coat a baking sheet with cooking spray. Mix dry ingredients, sifting together the flour, sugar, baking powder, and salt. Cut the butter and cream cheese into the dry ingredients until the mixture resembles coarse crumbs. In a separate bowl, beat together milk and egg. Pour into the dry ingredients, stirring only until blended. (Don't overmix when adding dry and liquid ingredients, or the result will be tough scones.) Mix the chopped pecans into the dough. Divide the dough in half and form into 8-inch rounds on the baking sheet. With a sharp knife, cut the dough into 8 wedges. Using a pastry brush, brush the top of each round with milk. Sprinkle sugar on top.

Bake at 400 degrees for 10-12 minutes or until scones are lightly browned.

Note: My friend Debra, who is nicknamed the Scone Lady, taught me that the secret to making good scones is not handling the dough any more than you have to. Too much handling makes the scones hard.

DEVONSHIRE CREAM

1 cup whipping cream
4 tablespoons powdered sugar
1 tablespoon orange juice
1/2 carton sour cream

With an electric mixer, beat whipping cream until soft peaks form. Blend in orange juice, sour cream, and powdered sugar. Keep refrigerated, for it will only keep unrefrigerated for a few hours.

CANDY STRAWBERRIES

Makes: 48

    2 6-ounce boxes wild
        strawberry flavor Jell-O
    2 cups pecans, chopped
    1 can Eagle Brand sweetened
        condensed milk
    2 cups flaked coconut

*Mix all of the ingredients together and
form dough into 1-inch balls. In a plastic
container (use one with a tight-sealing
lid), mix 1 cup granulated sugar with
2 drops red food coloring. Put the lid
on and shake vigorously to color the
sugar. Drop the balls into the sugar mix
and, with the lid on, shake vigorously to
coat them in sugar. Take balls out and,
with your fingertips, form them into
strawberry shapes. Place on a cookie
sheet lined with wax paper. Press in
a pecan sliver for a stem or use ready-
made decorative green icing and press
a leaf on each "strawberry." Let dry
for several hours on wax paper.
Store in an airtight
container.*

TEA PARTY BUTTER COOKIES *Makes: 24*

My mother used to make
these for my doll and me
to have tea parties with when I was
growing up. Children love these
easy-bake cookies!

    1 cup butter
    1 cup sugar
    1/4 teaspoon salt
    1 large egg
    1 teaspoon pure vanilla extract
    2 cups all-purpose flour

*In a large mixing bowl, cream together
butter, sugar, and salt. Add egg, vanilla,
and flour, mixing well. Drop a scant
teaspoonful of dough onto a nonstick
cookie sheet. Place a pecan half in the
center of each cookie. Bake at 350
degrees for 10 minutes.*

LONG-LASTING FLOWERS

A friend of mine who owns a floral shop gave me some tips worth remembering for making your cut flowers last longer.

TRIM AND TRIM AGAIN

Cut flowers often wilt because a buildup of bacteria "clogs" the stems. To keep the flowers taking in water, trim stems one-quarter inch before you first put them in water. To keep them lasting even longer, trim stems again every two to three days.

FEED THEM

Flowers need food for energy, but because the flowers have been cut they cannot get food from the plant. Most florists carry a packaged preservative that you can simply add to the water. My easy homemade mixture is one part water with one part lemon-lime drink. Avoid diet drinks, for they lack the sugar that flowers need.

CHANGE THE WATER

Bacteria grow especially fast if you feed the flowers. Change the water and keep it sparkling clean. One or two teaspoons of bleach, depending on the size of the vase, also helps to eliminate the problem.

KEEP THEM COOL

Avoid putting your flowers near direct sunlight or home heat sources, for heat speeds up the wilting process. If possible, set flowers outside in the cool night air or place them in the refrigerator overnight, all the while making sure the temperature doesn't dip below freezing.

The true essentials of a feast
are only fun and feed.

OLIVER WENDELL HOLMES

Come Gather at My Table in the Summer

Independence Day seems to be the highlight of our summer, but family reunions, weddings, and class reunions are all wonderful occasions to fire up the grill and host an outdoor gathering. Our family likes to cook out so much that we built a complete outdoor kitchen this year! Having a backyard barbecue means that nobody has to slave away cooking inside and miss all the fun outside.

Whether it is hamburgers on the grill for the softball team or grilled chicken for my nephew's wedding party, foods seem to taste most delicious when they are eaten at a table of grace out-of-doors. When the days grow long and early summer magnolia blossoms beckon me to draw near, even the simplest of meals becomes an occasion in itself when it is eaten out-of-doors.

At the peak of summer, gardens spring forth in abundance. Some days I come home to find a sack of okra on my back doorstep. Sometimes it is a bag of fresh green beans, and sometimes it is an array of cucumbers and tomatoes. My neighbor down the road has a huge garden, and it is his joy to share it with the neighbors.

Both Mason and Samuel each have their own garden spot. They always race to see who will have the first tomatoes or the first cucumbers. And they are so disappointed if I don't come up with a way to use all of the tomatoes that their gardens yield.

> **When one has tasted watermelon, one knows what the angels eat.**
>
> MARK TWAIN

I love to plant and tend my herb garden. Ripe tomatoes, a slice of fresh mozzarella, a bit of fresh basil—this is the essence of summer for me. With the abundance of tomatoes we usually have, I love making big batches of gazpacho. It keeps nicely in the fridge for days and, served cold, is quite refreshing on a hot, Southern summer day.

Our state, Arkansas, is well-known for its watermelons. In fact, we have a watermelon festival every summer! Red, yellow, big, little, and now even seedless—watermelons come in all shapes and sizes. Deep red melons with dark green outer shells are my personal favorites for flavor. For our outdoor parties, it is so fun to make a watermelon punch bowl. My recipe for punch is easy and tastes delightful for all ages. If time doesn't allow me to carve a watermelon punch bowl for my outdoor party, I get out my son's little red wagon that he has long outgrown and fill it with ice, canned drinks, and bottled water. It looks festive and it's portable, as I am able to move it anywhere in the garden.

After I complimented him on his beautiful table, the executive chef at the Ritz-Carlton told me, "We eat with our eyes." I know that even for my table at home, presentation marks the difference between an ordinary meal and a celebration of food. That little bit of extra effort can make a meal so much more appetizing and memorable. And it can easily be something that I already have on hand. When summertime vegetables are in abundance, they become my serving pieces. A red cabbage carved out in the middle holds dip. Red, green, and yellow bell peppers can hold a trio of dips. A cantaloupe cut in half and hollowed out is a perfect bowl for fruit salad. A pineapple split in half lengthwise can hold chicken salad. It all depends on the season's bounty and my own imagination.

My favorite flowers of summer are full-blooming florals for languid Southern summer afternoons—magnolia, lilac, gardenia. These flowers look especially pretty floating in a bowl of water as a table centerpiece or in an indoor fountain. I have a tabletop water fountain that is small enough to use on a buffet table. The sound of the water is cooling and soothing. The flowers floating in the water add a romantic atmosphere to a summer evening.

In the summer, I love to use my collection of earthenware crocks, white enameled dishpans, white oak handmade baskets, and galvanized pails for outdoor tableware. I painted my mother's old ten-gallon pickling crock with lemons, ribbons, and lemon leaves, and now it is my urn to serve lemonade in. With strawberries and sliced lemons floating in the lemonade, family and friends find it pretty too. I use Mother's old enamel dipper for a ladle and drape a dishcloth over the top to keep any unwanted bugs or twigs out of the lemonade.

Decorations are so easy with a summertime party. We fly a full-size American flag most days by our door, and always in the summer. I also like to place small American flags in my pots of impatiens, petunias, and geraniums that line the patio. Flowers blooming, flags flying— any meal outdoors instantly becomes festive!

FOURTH OF JULY PARTY MENU

Lemonade

Fruit Punch in a Watermelon
Punch Bowl

Gazpacho Dip with Corn Chips

Deviled Eggs

So-Easy Barbecue Chicken

Ranch-Style Potatoes

Grill-Roasted Corn
with Herbed Butter

Pineapple Boat Fruit Salad

Black-Eyed Pea Salad

Southern Blackberry Cobbler
with Homemade Ice Cream

WATERMELON PUNCH BOWL

I enjoy a beautiful punch bowl from nature when I use a real watermelon to serve my punch in. Choose a large, ripe watermelon that balances nicely. Cut the top off and scoop out the melon. Freeze the outside shell for 2-3 hours. Place the shell on a large oval platter surrounded by fresh flowers. Add your favorite fruit punch and serve it from the Watermelon Punch Bowl. Make melon balls with the meat from the watermelon and use them in a fruit salad.

GAZPACHO DIP

Serves: 12

Gazpacho served with corn chips is a great way to begin a party. It lets guests nibble while you finish up the meal. Cool and spicy with fresh basil and cilantro from Mason's garden, this recipe is one of our summertime favorites. Make this the day before you plan to serve it to let the flavors blend together.

1 large can tomato juice
1 8-ounce can tomato sauce
12 small-to-medium, vine-ripe tomatoes, coarsely chopped
1 tablespoon olive oil
1/4 cup apple cider vinegar
2 4-ounce cans diced chilies
1 4-ounce can sliced black olives
1 clove garlic, minced
1/4 pound mushrooms, cleaned and sliced

1 large cucumber, peeled and diced
6 green onions, finely chopped
1 teaspoon fresh basil, finely chopped
3 teaspoons cilantro, finely chopped
juice of 1 lime
1 teaspoon cumin
1 teaspoon paprika
1 teaspoon garlic salt
1 teaspoon coarsely ground pepper

In a large bowl, mix all ingredients together. Keep in fridge until ready to serve. Serve with king-size corn chips for dipping.

Note: When serving a large crowd, I like to put my Gazpacho Dip in a large serving bowl. I set it down on top of a large dishpan filled with ice so that the dip stays cool.

DEVILED EGGS

Makes: 24

    12 hard-cooked eggs
    1/4 cup mayonnaise
    3 tablespoons Thousand Island
        dressing
    4 tablespoons spicy brown
        mustard
    1/4 teaspoon garlic salt
    1 tablespoon pickle relish,
        finely chopped
    dash of black pepper
    paprika
    sliced black olives (for garnish)
    chives (for garnish)

*Slice eggs in half and remove yolks.
Place whites on the tray you plan to
serve eggs on. Mash yolks in a mixing
bowl and mix with mayonnaise,
Thousand Island dressing, mustard,
garlic salt, relish, and a dash of black
pepper. Refill the egg white halves with
yolk mix. Sprinkle each one with a
dash of paprika. Garnish half of the
eggs with sliced black olives. On the
remaining eggs, tie a bow from a blade
of chives to garnish the tops.*

SO-EASY BARBECUE CHICKEN

This can be made in the oven
or on the grill.

    1/4 cup margarine
    1 package dry onion soup mix
    1 cup hickory-flavored
        barbecue sauce
    1 chicken breast for each
        person

*Oven Method: Preheat oven to 350
degrees. Melt the margarine in the preheating oven in a rectangular casserole
dish. In a small bowl, mix onion soup
with barbecue sauce. Add melted butter.
Brush both sides of the chicken with
the sauce and bake uncovered at 350
degrees for 1 hour.*

*Grill Method: In a small mixing bowl,
melt butter in the microwave. Add
barbecue sauce and onion soup mix.
Stir to blend. Using a pastry brush,
baste chicken on both sides with
the sauce. Save remaining sauce for
basting while the chicken is grilling.
Grill until chicken is done.*

RANCH-STYLE POTATOES *Serves: 4–6*

1 package frozen potato
    nuggets
1/2 cup vegetable oil
3 1/4-ounce packages
    ranch-style salad dressing
    mix

Preheat oven to 450 degrees. Place
potatoes in single layers on 2 baking
sheets. In a mixing bowl, combine the
oil and dressing mix. Whisk until
blended. Drizzle dressing mix over the
two pans of potatoes. Bake for 15–20
minutes.

GRILL-ROASTED CORN WITH HERBED BUTTER

At the market, choose corn in the husks that is fresh and has not dried out or turned brown. My mother's method adds bacon drippings. Now that we are all trying to eat much healthier, bacon drippings may be omitted.

1 ear of corn for each person
1 stick butter, melted
1/4 cup hot bacon drippings
    (may be omitted)
1 teaspoon fresh rosemary,
    finely chopped
1 teaspoon fresh thyme, finely
    chopped

Peel back the husks on the corn, still
leaving them attached. Remove the silk
and rinse well. With a paper towel, pat
corn dry. In a small mixing bowl, mix
melted butter and fresh herbs. With a
pastry brush, slather butter and herb
mix on corn. Fold back down the
husks and roast corn on top of the
grill for about 15 minutes.
Turn with tongs every so
often until corn is tender.

BLACK-EYED PEA SALAD *Serves: 12*

3 cans black-eyed peas
1 can cut green beans
1 cup small cauliflower florets
1 small red onion, sliced and
   separated into rings
6 cherry tomatoes, halved
1/4 cup sweet red pepper,
   coarsely chopped
1/2 cup olive oil
1/2 cup white vinegar
1 clove garlic, finely chopped
1 teaspoon chili powder
1/2 teaspoon salt
1/4 teaspoon coarsely ground
   black pepper
leafy salad greens

In a large bowl, combine black-eyed peas, green beans, cauliflower, onion rings, cherry tomatoes, and red peppers. In a second bowl, whisk together oil, vinegar, garlic, chili powder, salt, and black pepper. Pour the dressing over the black-eyed pea mixture and toss until peas are well coated. Refrigerate in an airtight container until ready to serve. When ready to serve, line a serving bowl with salad greens. Spoon salad in the center of the greens. Be sure to refrigerate any leftovers.

SOUTHERN BLACKBERRY COBBLER

Serves: 8

This recipe from my mother is so wonderful that I usually double it!

4 heaping cups blackberries,
   freshly washed
1 1/2 cups granulated sugar
1/2 cup butter
3/4 cup self-rising flour
3/4 cup milk

Melt butter in 8" x 12" glass baking dish while preheating oven to 350 degrees. Mix together sugar, flour, and milk. Pour mixture over melted butter in baking dish. Spread blackberries over the mixture and bake at 350 degrees for 1 hour.

PINEAPPLE BOAT FRUIT SALAD *Serves: 12*

6 ripe pineapples
12 cups watermelon balls
12 kiwi fruit, peeled and sliced
1 cup fresh blueberries
4 starfruit, sliced

1/2 cup flaked coconut
1 cup lime juice
1 cup sugar
fresh mint (for garnish)

Cut pineapples in half lengthwise. Make two cuts on the diagonal to score a deep "V" down the middle of the pineapple. Pull out this section to remove the core. With a grapefruit knife, cut around the edges to pull out the fruit and leave a pineapple bowl intact. Slice the pineapple fruit into bite-size pieces. In a large mixing bowl, combine pineapple pieces, watermelon balls, kiwi, blueberries, starfruit, and coconut. In a separate bowl, mix lime juice and sugar. Whisk until sugar is completely dissolved. Pour over fruit mixture and refrigerate until time to serve. When ready to serve, spoon into pineapple boats. Garnish each boat with a sprig of mint.

Note: If you are making this a bit ahead of time, you can store the scooped-out pineapple shells on a cookie sheet in the refrigerator. Drape a damp paper towel over them to keep them fresh.

The cheerful joyous season
The Autumn time is come.
With song and shout we welcome
The Golden Harvest Home.

AUTHOR UNKNOWN

Come Gather at My Table in the Autumn

The days grow short, the air has a chill to it, and the pumpkins swell on the vine. A new school year begins and friendships are rekindled. Autumn is a time of gathering in, whether we are gathering fresh-picked apples or gathering with faraway relatives. Autumn is a celebration of the harvest. It is a time for bringing out the quilts, draping them over rocking chairs to create a cozy spot, and enjoying a mug of hot spiced cider underneath the golden glow of the harvest moon.

Wise are they who can make the little moment as it comes and make it brighter ere 'tis gone.

A SHAKER PROVERB

Golden October's morn and gray November's skies call for tables set with tradition. From the celebration of an early fall harvest to the Thanksgiving holidays, there is no season that calls us home like this one does.

To celebrate the harvest season, our family hosts a Fall Fling the last weekend in October. We build a campfire near the grand old cedar tree that graces our pasture. My husband readies the John Deere tractor and hitches up the old wooden trailer, which has been piled high with hay. I make a "Kodak picture spot" with a homemade scarecrow and bales of hay decorated with bright yellow mums. The clear mountain lake is the backdrop for this memorable picture—and party. The canoe awaits a taker. The enamel coffeepot is brimming with hot chocolate. Bales of hay draped with vintage tablecloths and quilts circle the campfire and dot the lawn for seating. I thrill as our guests begin to arrive, for the smell of fall is in the air.

> *Glad memories link days gone by with those that are to come.*
>
> ALDA

If you are not able to build a campfire at home, you can host your gathering at a park with a campfire area. But if you really want to have your dinner at home, gather 'round a chiminea—a large, terra-cotta "outdoor fireplace." They come in all sizes, and most any porch or patio will do. Even if your "outdoors" is an apartment balcony and you have no place to burn wood, you can place a large, three-wick candle or several column candles of different heights inside the chiminea. We love to gather round our chiminea, especially on our Sunday night soup supper to savor the last meal of the weekend. It is amazing how much heat they can put out, and they roast marshmallows quite nicely!

HARVEST CAMPFIRE DINNER

Ozark Mountain Cheese Soup
Pumpkin Bread
Roasted Hot Dogs
Butterscotch Brownies
Roasted Marshmallows
Wagon Wheel Cider

PUMPKIN BREAD

Makes: 3 loaves

3 1/2 cups all-purpose flour, sifted
2 teaspoons baking soda
1 1/2 teaspoons salt
2 teaspoons cinnamon
2 teaspoons nutmeg
3 1/2 cups sugar
4 eggs, beaten
2/3 cup water
1 cup salad oil
2 cups (1 16-ounce can) pumpkin puree
1 cup pecans, chopped
2/3 cup raisins

Combine flour, baking soda, salt, cinnamon, nutmeg, and sugar in a large mixing bowl. Add eggs, water, oil, and pumpkin. Stir until blended. Add nuts and raisins. Mix well. Pour mixture into 3 buttered and floured loaf pans or 3 1-pound coffee cans. Bake at 350 degrees for 1 hour. Cool slightly. Turn out on wire rack to finish cooling. For best flavor, bake pumpkin bread at least a day before it is to be served. Store covered in refrigerator or freezer. Serve with softened cream cheese.

OZARK MOUNTAIN CHEESE SOUP

Serves: 8

> 1/2 cup margarine
> 1/2 cup onions, finely minced
> 1/4 cup carrot, grated
> 1/4 cup celery, finely chopped
> 1/2 cup flour
> 2 tablespoons cornstarch
> 1 quart clear chicken stock
> 1 quart milk
> 2 1/2 cups Velveeta cheese,
>   shredded
> washed dandelion leaves
>   (for garnish)

In a small skillet, sauté onions, carrots, and celery. In a large saucepan, cream together flour and cornstarch. Pour in chicken stock and milk. Stir and cook until thickened. Add sautéed ingredients and cheese. Cover and simmer on low for 1 hour. Season with salt and pepper. Garnish with a dandelion leaf or edible blossom just before serving.

WAGON WHEEL CIDER   *Makes: 1 gallon*

I like to collect old thermoses from tag sales so that every person or couple can have their own thermos of hot cider.

> 1 gallon apple cider
> 1 cup light brown sugar
> 4 2-inch cinnamon sticks
> 1 teaspoon whole allspice
> 2 teaspoons whole cloves

Pour apple juice into a clean (no coffee!) 30-cup electric, percolator-style coffeepot. Pour the cider in the urn and put the basket in place. Drop the cinnamon, sugar, and spices into the basket and let perk as usual. Serve hot, with a cinnamon stick in each thermos or mug.

Note: For a take-home favor, a thoughtful present is a cheerful mug with homemade or packaged instant cocoa or cider tucked inside. Wrap mugs in fabric scraps of country plaid and tie on a ribbon with a hangtag that reads: "A Hug in a Cup." Make a memory that will last!

In the other gardens
And all up the vale,
From autumn bonfires
See the smoke trail!

Pleasant summer over
And all the summer flowers,
The red fire blazes,
The gray smoke towers.

ROBERT LOUIS
STEVENSON

BUTTERSCOTCH BROWNIES

Makes: 30 brownies

    2 6-ounce packages butterscotch bits
    1/2 cup butter
    4 eggs
    1 cup light brown sugar
    1 1/2 cups all-purpose flour, sifted
    1 1/4 teaspoons salt
    1 teaspoon baking powder
    2 cups walnuts or pecans, chopped

*Melt butterscotch bits with butter in the top of a double boiler. Remove
from heat. Beat eggs with sugar in a large bowl with an electric mixer until
light and fluffy. Sift in flour, salt, and baking powder; beat until blended.
Add melted butterscotch mixture, then stir in nuts. Pour into lightly greased
15" x 10" x 1" jellyroll pan and bake at 350 degrees for 25 minutes.
Cool and cut into squares.*

Come, ye thankful people, come,
Raise the song of harvest home;
All is safely gathered in,
Ere the winter storms begin.

HENRY ALFORD

Come Gather at My Table in the Winter

For large gatherings during the winter holidays, a buffet is a favorite way to entertain, for it is very adaptable. The word *buffet* is actually the name of a piece of furniture, usually used in the dining room. We have seen its meaning evolve, for *buffet* has turned into a common term for "serving yourself." The number of guests is not so crucial, and timing is easier, for it allows flexibility in everyone's schedule— including the hostess. When it is a "drop-in" buffet, guests find it easier to work this kind of party into their busy holiday calendar.

The secret to a good buffet is in the planning—planning a menu, planning a shopping list, planning the layout of your table, even planning what foods can be kept warm over an extended period of time and what foods need to be kept cold. In all of this planning, I look for foods that can be made ahead of time. If I see a good recipe but note that it cannot be made the day before, I turn the page. It may be a great recipe, but it is not great for my buffet.

I always try to plan the placement of the food and drinks to make serving easy. For instance, I place the dinner plates at one end of the buffet, with silverware and napkins on the opposite end. By doing so, guests don't have to fumble with their plates while trying to hold onto silverware. It also keeps the line moving smoothly and prevents guests from having to backtrack. Drinks are usually served in a separate area, or at least on the other side of the room. This helps to keep any one area from becoming too congested.

In announcing a buffet dinner ready to serve, I casually hand a guest a plate from the beginning of the buffet table and ask, "Will you start the line for me?" Most guests follow without having to be asked, and your party has begun!

As the party winds down to the last remaining guests, someone dear will always say to me, "I can't leave you with all these dishes. It will only take a minute if I help." With much appreciation, I always warmly refuse, for I want to enjoy my guests' company while they are with me. My mother used to do this to me sometimes, and I would always feel guilty as she kindly refused my offer to help. Now I understand what she was doing. Party clothes do not need to be made a mess of, and I actually enjoy the cleaning-up part in some unexplained way. After the guests have left, I change into something comfortable—with especially comfortable shoes—and savor pulling

the dishes together and loading the dishwasher. Handling my good crystal, china, and silver and caring for them are part of the joy of having beautiful possessions. In the quiet of the aftermath, it is a perfect time to savor who came, who was missing, what was a big success, and what I would do differently the next time.

The key to having a successful party is seeing to it that everyone else has a good time, and the hostess seems to end up having a better time than anybody. No matter if it is a small family gathering or a party for two hundred, if I have tried to see that each person's needs have been met while they were in my care, I have offered them a table of grace.

It is my prayer that your table of grace, filled with new acquaintances, old friends, or loved ones, will bring you love, joy, peace, hope, and all that is good.

HOLIDAY OPEN HOUSE

Sparkling Fruit Tea
Candy Cane Cookies
Tupelo Cheese Ball
Southern Glazed Pecans
White Chocolate Holiday Fudge
Date Nut Log
Apricot Balls
Pistachio Nut Torte
Christmas Punch

SPARKLING FRUIT TEA *Serves: 12*

4 cups water
16 orange-spice flavored
    tea bags
1 cup sugar
1 can frozen apple juice
    concentrate, thawed
1 large bottle sparkling white
    grape juice, very chilled

Bring 4 cups of water to a boil. Remove from heat and steep tea bags in hot water for 10 minutes. Add sugar, stirring until dissolved. In a 1-gallon pitcher, mix apple juice concentrate and water. Stir in the tea. Chill well. When it is time to serve, add grape juice to the tea and garnish with a slice of lemon.

APRICOT BALLS

Makes: 36

16 ounces ground apricots
1 can sweetened condensed
    milk
3 cups flaked coconut
2 cups powdered sugar

In a large mixing bowl, mix apricots, milk, and coconut. Roll mixture into 1-inch balls in the palm of your hand. Place powdered sugar in a separate bowl. Drop the apricot balls into the powdered sugar and coat well. Place on wax paper and dry completely before storing in a covered container.

TUPELO CHEESE BALL

My Aunt Wese makes this especially for me every year when I spend the holidays in her home. One year she made a different cheese ball and said, "I will never do that again!" This one is just the best.

> 2 8-ounce packages
>   cream cheese
> 1 8 1/2-ounce can
>   crushed pineapple
> 1/4 cup green bell pepper,
>   chopped
> 2 cups pecans, chopped
> 2 tablespoons green onion,
>   chopped
> 1 teaspoon salt

Beat cream cheese until smooth. Add drained pineapple and 1 cup of pecans. Add remaining ingredients (except second cup of pecans). Shape into a ball and roll in remaining cup of pecans. Chill overnight. Serve with crackers.

CANDY CANE COOKIES

Makes: 4 dozen cookies

> 1 cup shortening
> 1 cup confectioner's sugar,
>   sifted
> 1 egg
> 1 1/2 teaspoons almond extract
> 1 teaspoon vanilla
> 2 1/2 cups all-purpose flour
> 1 teaspoon salt
> 1/2 teaspoon red food
>   coloring
> 1/2 cup peppermint candies,
>   crushed
> 1/2 cup granulated sugar

Preheat oven to 375 degrees. Mix shortening, sugar, egg, and flavorings thoroughly. Sift flour and salt; stir into shortening mixture. Divide dough in half. Blend red food coloring into half of dough. Roll 4-inch strips (using about a teaspoon of dough for each strip) from each color. Form smooth, even strips, rolling them back and forth on a lightly floured board. Twist strips like rope and crook ends to make canes. Place on an ungreased cookie sheet. Bake for about 9 minutes or until light brown. When still warm, sprinkle with mixture of candy and sugar.

SOUTHERN GLAZED PECANS

H ere in Arkansas, we always have an abundance of pecans. As a
Thanksgiving gift, my favorite uncle always ushers me out to the
barn and hands me a large grocery sack filled with pecans, cracked and
ready to shell. My aunt and uncle have several stately towering pecan trees
in their yard. Still, every tiny pecan has to be picked up by hand. So this gift
is, I know, truly a labor of love. I take the sack of pecans home and pour the
nuts out into one of my white enameled dishpans and set it next to my
husband's chair. As the darkness of the evening arrives early in the fall, he
watches the news on television and picks out the pecans for me. There is
always enough so we can nibble on some now and freeze more for later.
Pecan pies, pumpkin bread—all sorts of good things come out of that
brown paper sack of pecans, including this recipe.

2 cups shelled pecans
1/2 cup butter
1/4 cup light corn syrup
salt

*Spread pecans evenly in a 8 1/2" x 13" aluminum baking pan. Scatter butter
in pats over nuts, then drizzle with corn syrup. Roast in a slow oven—
which is the Southern way of saying "a low temperature, yet
watchful eye"—at 250 degrees.*

*Stir occasionally until slightly browned (about
1 hour). Add extra butter if spoon
becomes sticky when stirring. Line
counter with brown grocery sack
paper. Spread roasted nuts on paper
and salt generously, tossing nuts to
make sure that all are covered.*

DATE NUT LOG

40 graham cracker squares,
    divided and finely crushed
24 large marshmallows,
    snipped (or 1 bag
    miniature marshmallows)
8 ounces chopped dates
2 cups pecans
1 1/4 cups heavy cream

*In a large mixing bowl, combine 2 cups
of graham cracker crumbs, marshmallows,
dates, and pecans. Stir in cream and
mix well. Shape into a 12" x 3" log.
Roll to coat in remaining graham cracker
crumbs. Wrap in plastic wrap and
refrigerate overnight. Garnish with
red and green candied cherries.*

*Note: Place graham crackers in a Ziploc
bag with the air let out. Roll over them
with a rolling pin to crush.*

PISTACHIO NUT TORTE

Serves: 12

Crust:

1 cup flour
1/2 cup butter, melted
1/4 cup pecans, chopped
4 tablespoons sugar

*Mix flour, butter, pecans, and sugar
together. Press into a 9" x 12" baking
dish. Bake at 325 degrees for 15
minutes. Let cool.*

Filling:

8 ounces cream cheese,
    softened
1 cup powdered sugar
1 12-ounce container
    whipped topping
2 3-ounce packages instant
    pistachio flavored pudding
    mix
2 1/2 cups milk

*Mix cream cheese, powdered
sugar, and 1/2 of whipped
topping. Beat well and spread
over cooled crust. Mix
together pudding and milk.
Pour over cream mixture
and top with remaining
whipped topping. Refrigerate
at least 2 hours before serving.*

CHRISTMAS PUNCH
Serves: 20

G rowing up, this punch was always a Christmas Eve tradition at our house. My sister, aunt, and I have made it a part of our Thanksgiving and Christmas gatherings too. It is so good, yet so easy to make. When we are asked for the recipe, it is almost embarrassing to tell, for it is just too simple! You don't even need an ice ring, for the sherbet keeps the punch cold.

> 2 2-liter bottles ginger ale (almost frozen)
> 1/2 gallon lime sherbet

Pour ginger ale into cooled punch bowl. Scoop out sherbet and place in bowl. Stir slightly.

Note: For bridesmaids' luncheons and birthday parties, raspberry sherbet and orange sherbet look very pretty. Pineapple sherbet, which is white in color, is perfect for weddings and anniversaries.

WHITE CHOCOLATE HOLIDAY FUDGE
Makes: 16 one-inch squares

> 2 cups granulated sugar
> 3/4 cup sour cream
> 1/2 cup butter
> 12 ounces white chocolate pieces
> 1 7-ounce jar marshmallow cream
> 1/2 cup pecan pieces, coarsely chopped
> 1/2 cup green candied cherries
> 1/2 cup red candied cherries

In a heavy saucepan, mix sugar, sour cream, and butter, bringing mixture to a rolling boil. Stir constantly so it does not stick to bottom of pan. Boil for 7 minutes over medium heat while continuing to stir. Remove from heat and stir in white chocolate pieces until melted. Add remaining ingredients.

Spray an 8-inch baking pan with nonstick coating. Pour mixture into baking pan. Let cool before cutting into 1-inch squares.